Me

Shepherd King

By Ronnie Guynes

Table of Contents

Acknowledgments

This book was written for those who seek to understand the depth of the divine and the mysteries unveiled in His presence.

I'm especially thankful to my parents, whose life lessons I continue to learn from daily.

To my children: Micah, Courtney and Corrie, and to my granddaughter, Kennedy—you are my joy and inspiration.

To my best friend, my wife for life: Linda—thank you for your support in all the missions in which God has called me to serve.

Finally, thanks to my friend, David Yeazell, for your encouragement and support during the writing of this book.

A Note From The Author

Of all the sixty-six books of the Bible, the Book of Psalms is considered one of the most popular. Long used as a resource for personal devotion and corporate worship, it holds a unique and profound message for all.

Originally composed as a collection of hymns, the lyrics of these songs continue to bring us comfort, encouragement, inspiration, peace, instruction and wisdom.

They could easily be described as "God's Music Room"—a rich compilation of classics birthed out of gritty, real life experience and deep testing, tragedy and loss, and victory and defeat. Through them, the Holy Spirit can touch the very strings of our hearts and fine-tune us to the faithfulness, character and wisdom of a great God.

The Psalms are commonly spoken of as "David's" because he is credited with writing the larger number of them (seventy-three are ascribed to him in their titles).

In David's youth he was more than a shepherd boy. Beyond exercising the skills needed to tend and protect his flock, David was also a poet, musician, and a minstrel.

While a musician can play an instrument, which results in the production of harmonic sounds, a minstrel allows God to prophesy through that instrument playing sounds that carry the anointing. That explains why

David would play his harp and demons would flee from Saul.

As we internalize the prophetic lyrics found within the Psalms of David, it becomes clear that the same powerful anointing that resided upon David as he wrote them lives on in everyone who embraces their message.

We are uniquely privileged that David allows us to observe the many phases of his life. We see him grow from an unknown shepherd boy to a servant in the King's palace—weighed down with problems, trials, and such heartache that he seeks a way of escape.

We follow his life as he matures and learns to encourage and remind himself of simpler days when he ran barefoot through the hills doing what he loved most—caring for his father's sheep.

He exposes to us the good, the bad, and even the ugly. We join him as he exalts the Living God in the highest form of praise; we identify with him as he repents in humility; and we hear his fear, his courage, and a myriad of emotions as he expresses himself in a vast array of poetic styles and expression.

Meditations of a Shepherd King is based on what is probably the most poignant of all the Psalms: the twenty-third. The chapters that follow will lead you, the reader, into a world of self-discovery—a world where you can identify with David's journey from obscurity to a place of promotion and honor.

Chapter One—
The Lord Is My Shepherd

"The Lord is my Shepherd" is a statement that evokes a thousand tender emotions for the one who understands the role of a shepherd in the life of his sheep, and has experienced the Lord's care in a similar manner.

David was a shepherd, learning his skill from his earthly father who also was a shepherd. Later in life, David carried the title as the "Shepherd King" of Israel.

In his relationship to the Lord, David constantly grasped for something tangible to illustrate the relationship between the human and the divine. He wrestled within himself to find adequate words to express this revelation knowledge. His experience as a shepherd to his father's sheep provided the inspiration he needed to relate the human/divine connection.

David had a great love for his sheep; he was willing to risk his life for them. He cared for them, singing songs for them in the night to calm them and make them feel totally secure.

With David's experience and understanding of what a good shepherd was, he got the revelation: "The Lord is my Shepherd." His voice thundered as he sang this statement and heard his own echo affirm again and again, "The Lord is my Shepherd."

Through this simple declaration, David spoke out of revelation knowledge and proclaimed God as his divine protector, provider and nurturer.

As David matured into adulthood he was transformed into a fearless warrior and became a wealthy and powerful king, yet eventually found himself exiled from his own people. At the peak of his popularity he became a fugitive running for his life.

The seas of life indeed tossed David from extreme highs to extreme lows—sometimes poor, sometimes rich; sometimes loved, sometimes hated; honored and persecuted, prominent and obscure, joyful and sad—David was intimately acquainted with life's unexpected turns and the fickleness of people.

That's why we find him constantly in the secret place with his harp bearing all to God, his only anchor of hope, the only one that could speak peace to his storm, "The LORD God All – Mighty!"

"The" Lord, not "a" lord or "one of the lords," but "The" Lord. There is only one Lord of all Lords and King of all Kings. There is one sovereign God who is ruler of the universe, "The King of Glory." No one can compare or compete with Him for He is all-powerful, all-knowing and ever-present.

God is Spirit, and, therefore, cannot be defined physically or intellectually. If we are to understand anything about God, He must first reveal Himself to us. Anything other than revelation is merely imagination.

As we enter the secret place through worship, the manifest presence of God reveals to us who He is. This diadem of royalty, this sovereign ruling monarch, this Creator of galaxies and ruler of the earth calls Himself my Shepherd. He also refers to Himself as "The Good Shepherd."

To know that the Lord is the Good Shepherd is to know contentment, security and peace. As we come to a place of full surrender we recognize that we truly belong to the loving Shepherd of our soul.

To say, "The Lord is my Shepherd" like David, I must understand the principles of ownership. It's one thing for someone to own me, but an entirely different matter to surrender to that ownership.

God owns me because without Him I would have no existence and without His input I would have no destiny. I am the workmanship of His hands, fashioned out of His heart's desire.

Our accomplishments may be found in what we do, but will only bring us temporary satisfaction. Our popularity may be found in who we are, but will only bring us temporary affirmation.

Our true significance can only be found in the One who made us. Our self-worth can only be defined by what God says about us.

Meditation for Today

I have great significance because I belong to the Lord. Just like sheep, I am totally dependent upon the Lord to provide for my household, to lead me, and to watch over me.

God not only has love or gives love—He is love. His love is expressed to me in each of His attributes. My Shepherd loves me with a love I cannot define—it must be experienced. And I can only experience it as it is revealed from faith to faith and from glory to glory.

I am honored to abide under the care of my Shepherd. I want the world to know, The Lord ... is my Shepherd.

Chapter Two—I Shall Not Want

God created us as a needy people so He could be the supplier of each need. The words, "I shall not want" do not merely deal with the basic needs common to both sheep and people. "I shall not want" speaks of a relationship of complete satisfaction—we are so cared for by the Good Shepherd that we have no wants—we have a fulfilled life.

Where there is life, there will be needs. David knew what it meant to be hungry and need food, to be tired and need rest, to be cold and need warmth, to be thirsty and need a drink of water.

Having a relationship with God does not eliminate the needs in our life; it makes provision for them. The beauty of our relationship with God is that we can have needs in our lives and still be spiritually fulfilled.

Our joy is not dependent upon having all our needs met. Like Paul and Silas, we could be chained to a prison wall and still have a song of joy in our heart.

Joy is different from happiness. Happiness comes from outward circumstances and is temporary. We get happy because of a new job or opportunity, a change in our circumstances or an accomplishment. We are happy for a season, but it eventually fades. Our job gets old, the opportunity passes, change becomes routine and accomplishment becomes history.

Joy, however, comes from within and is lasting. Joy is a fruit of the spirit not connected to outward circumstances. Joy can spring up out of our spirit-man like a river of living water. In any trial, opposition or adversity, joy can be present in our lives.

If you have ever traveled to a third-world country, you probably found certain segments of the population living in the worst conditions of poverty. Some with only the clothes on their backs; others living in shelters made from cardboard boxes without water or electricity; and oftentimes, starving adults and severely malnourished children.

Yet, in the most dismal of situations, I have discovered people who are full of joy. They laugh and have a deep love for their family. Joy is what sustains them in hope. Grateful people are fulfilled and joyful.

Many Christians preach and live a selfish gospel rather than a self-less life. Selfishness is the basis of all sin and is a motivation that will never be satisfied.

Our selfish needs are not legitimate needs. When God promises to meet our needs, His promise is focused on providing every thing we need to reach our divine destiny.

Throughout the Word of God we read of men and women of God in trials, sufferings and hardships. However, they found their purpose and had what they needed to walk in their divine destiny.

Meditation for Today

There is grace for the place—the place of God's destiny for you—and God will always equip us for what He is requiring us to do. Each time the Spirit of God convicts us, He is ready to empower us to obey.

For example: if the Spirit of God convicts me of a habit, addiction or sin, He will give me the ability to lay it down, repent and walk in righteousness. If God requires me to do something impossible, I can trust that He will empower me to fulfill His will.

Only God can do God's work. I must choose to obey Him. As mature believers we must come to a place in our Christian walk where all we want is the presence of God. We should rise in the morning with a deep desire to seek His face and, throughout the day, have an awareness of His presence, His love and guidance. When my attention and desire are completely upon God and His Kingdom, I SHALL NOT WANT...

Chapter Three—
He Maketh Me To Lie Down In Green Pastures

We often read this statement and think it means that God makes us rest (as if we will totally exhaust ourselves if God does not intervene and cause us to slow down).

The word "make" is not used here as a word of force, for God never forces us to do anything. We were created with a free will to respond to Him. The word "make" is used in the same way we would say, "he makes me laugh, or he makes me happy." This is not a forced condition—on the contrary, it is a created condition.

Sheep are very interesting animals. When they eat, they must stand on their feet. If a sheep is lying down and becomes hungry, even though the grass is inches away from its mouth, it will jump to its feet to begin eating.

The picture of a sheep lying down in a green pasture is a picture of perfect contentment. To say that my Shepherd makes me lie down in green pastures is to say He makes me so content that I have need of nothing. A whole field of green grass surrounds me but I am so content I just lie down.

When I think of perfect peace and contentment, I picture Jesus asleep in the boat while in the middle of a storm. He had no care, no fear, only trust and security that all was well.

If sheep have any fear at all, they become restless and anxious. They will not lie down because their instincts tell them to run. If they are pestered by flies and pests swarming around their heads, they will stand.

The devil loves to intimidate believers about the "What if's" of life—what if this or that happens. He and his demonic underlings strive to swarm around our heads, pestering and irritating the saints in a thousand little ways.

We must learn to run to the Shepherd. "Let God arise, let his enemies be scattered" (Psalms 68:1). God has a secret place for each believer to find rest for their soul.

God likens us to sheep because they are dependent upon their Shepherd. Sheep are not like other animals that establish a pecking order of who is in charge. Monkeys have leadership, dogs follow a lead dog, and other species establish their territory and position. However, sheep simply follow.

When danger is present, if one sheep is panicked and begins to run, they all run because they are followers. The reason sheep are so dependent is because they were not created to defend themselves. They do not have fangs like a snake or antlers like a deer, horns like a ram or teeth like a lion. Their only defense is to huddle together or run. They cannot fight on their own—they must trust someone to fight for them.

Meditation for Today

"The weapons of our warfare are not carnal, but mighty through God to the pulling down of strongholds" (2 Corinthians 10:4). Exodus 14:14 commands us to hold our peace and God will fight for us. He is the God of Battles.

God is my protector—His presence brings me to a place of peace. Even though I have a field of green grass (a world of opportunity) around me, I find my state of being content in Him alone. Like the apostle I want to say, "I know how to be abased, and I know how to abound" (Philippians 4:12a; NKJV). In other words, I have slept on the streets and I have slept in the king's guest room. He goes on to say, "Everywhere and in all things I have learned both to be full and to be hungry, both to abound and to suffer need" (Philippians 4:12b; NKJV).

Philippians 4:11 states: "not that I speak in regard to need, for I have learned in whatever state I am to be content" (NKJV). He makes me lie down in green pastures.

Chapter Four—
He Leadeth Me Beside The
Still Waters

He leads us. He is our leader. God is not confused. He knows exactly what He wants to accomplish in and through our lives. The challenge is not in God's leadership; it is found in our follow-ship. We must constantly surrender in obedience to His desire.

There are places God desires to lead us to that we do not feel comfortable going. Many times our logic and reasoning get in the way because we do not understand the ways of God. Other times our emotions interfere because we are insecure, fearful or sometimes motivated by our pride and selfishness.

The Word of God commands us to cast down every vain imagination and to bring every thought into captivity unto the obedience to Christ Jesus (2 Corinthians 10:5; Author Paraphrase).

Each morning as we rise to start a new day, we must crucify our self life. If we don't, our will continually reaches for power and control. Our only salvation is for our will to die and surrender to the will of God.

The Bible says we should reckon ourselves as dead. A dead man is not offended; a dead man does not retaliate; and a dead man has no opinion. This is the struggle of being a disciple of Jesus. To be a disciple, we must have discipline to walk according to the principles of righteousness.

The still water is a righteous place of God's presence. Once we realize that the water we have access to is Jesus, the "Living Water," we will run like the Psalmist's deer, panting after that water. Jesus is the only one who can quench our thirst and satisfy our soul.

David was very aware of how necessary water was for him and his sheep to survive. In the desert water is very hard to find. A good shepherd would have a strategic plan to water his sheep before they became faint and dehydrated. David had a deep appreciation for water.

Samuel, the Old Testament judge and prophet, records a time when David and his mighty men were in a stronghold while the garrison of the Philistines was in Bethlehem. David was thinking about the cool sweet water in Bethlehem's well. As he reminisced about his times at this well, he spoke aloud and said, "Oh, if someone could just bring me a drink from the well in Bethlehem near the gate."

Three of David's men heard this and, because they loved David, risked their lives, broke through the enemy line and brought a drink of water to David.

When David realized the sacrifice, loyalty and commitment of his men, he was overwhelmed.

The water became more than a thirst-quenching liquid—it became a symbol of love and self-sacrifice; at that point it became a gift.

In honor of the moment, David refused to drink the water to satisfy his own selfish need. Instead, he poured it out as a drink offering.

Meditation for Today

Jesus was at a well one day asking a Samaritan woman for a drink. Her reply was, "Why do you ask me to give you a drink? I'm a Samaritan and you are a Jew and Jews have nothing to do with us" (John 4:9; Author Paraphrase).

Jesus said, "If you knew the gift of God and who it is who says to you, 'give me a drink,' you would have asked Him and He would have given you Living Water" (John 4:10; Author Paraphrase). He goes on to say, "Whoever drinks of the water I shall give him will never thirst" (John 4:14: NKJV).

Jesus sacrificed His life to become the life-giving water that quenches our thirsty soul. Like David, we too should give honor and not drink to satisfy our own selfishness.

As we drink in the blessings and the promises, we drink in the benefits of being a believer, but sometimes fail to see the sacredness of what Christ has done to provide for us. Our thanksgiving should be an acknowledgement of reverent appreciation.

"He leads me beside the still waters." He is the only one who can lead me to my destiny and give me life eternal. I choose this day to follow and obey His will for my life.

Chapter Five—
He Restoreth My Soul

It would seem that living under the protection and provision of a Good Shepherd would eliminate the need for restoration. However, being a believer does not exempt us from trials and tribulation. But with every trial we have the promise from God that He will never leave or forsake us.

David intimately knew the touch of restoration in his life. As a boy he was shunned by his brothers. When Samuel came to anoint one of Jesse's sons, David was not considered by his family. Later, David was treated unjustly and unfairly by King Saul. Throughout his life, David could have grown bitter and hard but he cried out to his Good Shepherd to restore him.

David loved the presence of God so deeply. He guarded his heart to abide in the life of God.

In one of the Psalms, David proclaims, "Create in me a clean heart, O God; and renew a right spirit within me. Cast me not away from thy presence; and take not thy holy spirit from me. Restore unto me the joy of thy Salvation…" (Psalm 51: 10, 11, 12a).

There will be many times that life will seem unfair: friends will betray, false accusers will create lies about us and people we trust will hurt us. If we respond to these issues in a negative way we become the loser.

Some people say, "But I have a right to be mad," or "I have a right to be bitter." Yes, you do have a right.

However, to continue in the presence and blessing of God you must relinquish your rights and trust God to deal with each situation in His justice, for He is a "Just God."

We hurt ourselves when we choose to retaliate and attack. When Jesus was standing before the authorities He did not say a word. He knew that people had lied about Him. He knew that He had done no wrong. In fact, He had lived His life to do well.

The Bible states that Jesus did not respond to His accusers. The description states He was like a lamb being led to the slaughter and yet He kept silent (Isaiah 53:7; Author Paraphrase).

Jesus kept silent—not because He had great willpower or because He was a great man of prayer—but because He knew who He was. He knew He was the only begotten Son of God. Jesus did not need to defend Himself or God. When you know who you truly are in Christ it does not matter what people think. What matters is how you respond to what people think.

If we allow ourselves to become bitter, unforgiving, angry and hateful we hurt our relationship with God. We might win a battle or get our point across but we lose the presence of God in the process.

When people attack our life and character or when circumstances seem unfair, we must roll each care over to the Lord and allow the Good Shepherd to restore us. He will deal with our enemies and our accusers.

When we relinquish our rights and choose God's way

we walk under the canopy of His Love. Our joy can be full to overflowing even in the darkest hour.

Through every storm, every trial, every heartache, "He restores my soul."

Meditation for Today

A definition of "restoration" is to re-condition, or re-build something to its original condition, purpose or function.

As God restores us, He returns us to the place where we discover the reason for which we were created: to live in the center of His Will, so we can fulfill His purpose and plan for our lives.

Chapter Six—
He Leadeth Me In The Paths Of Righteousness For His Name's Sake

The Bible states that "The steps of a good man are ordered by the Lord" (Psalms 37:23). The word "ordered" means ordained. God has ordained a path that we are to walk in. This path is not meant to be mystical and secretive. It is a revealed path that the Shepherd leads us on. Only God can show us what His plan is.

Many times we deviate from our path because we fail to seek God, we choose our own way or the enemy deceives us. The devil lays entrapments along the path to lure us away from our destiny. There are three reasons why the enemy does not want us to reach our destiny. First, he knows if we reach our destiny we obey the Will of God, so he tries to convince us to disobey.

Second, the devil knows by reaching our destiny we fulfill the will of God and therefore we too come to a place of fulfillment.

Third, if the will of God is obeyed and we are fulfilled in our purpose, then God is glorified.

The devil does all he can to neutralize us, stop us, or derail us so we fail to obey the will of God.

The devil's resistance is not about us. The devil is not afraid of us; he is trying to stop the Word of God from flowing through us. If he cannot stop us from being a vessel used by God, he will try to defile us through compromise and sin. Satan knows it is God's truth that sets the captives free.

We must strive to uphold a standard of holiness, guarding the glory of God's presence in our lives.

The path the Shepherd is leading us on is a path of blessing and prosperity. We must trust our Shepherd completely, for we walk by faith and not by sight. Sometimes on this path of life we will not be able to see all things clearly. That is when we put our trust in the One who leads us, for we know He loves us and desires to see us blessed.

I like what David reveals when he says, "He leadeth me in the paths of righteousness for His name's sake." For His name's sake—that name that is above every name.

Proverbs declares that, "The name of the Lord is a strong tower, the righteous run to it and are safe" (Proverbs 18:10; NKJV). The name of the Lord is much more than a title. Name means nature. The name of the Lord represents His character and His attributes. All that He is is expressed in His name.

Meditation for Today

Our God is a God of Covenant, and throughout the Bible you will read terms of Covenant. Each time God reveals one of His names He is establishing a Covenant. In other words, when God told Abraham He would be a friend, from that moment on God would be a friend not only to Abraham, but to all who came into covenant relationship with Him.

The name of a King encompasses all that he is or has. His name includes his kingdom, power, wealth, the strength of his army, and his honor or reputation.

So each name of God reveals to us another part of His glory. Our God is multi-faceted and we could never exhaust the revelation of who He is.

From faith to faith, from glory to glory, throughout eternity God will continue to reveal to us His radiant glory.

Jesus said, "And whatever you ask in My name, that I will do, that the Father may be glorified in the Son" (John 14:13; NKJV). Ask in "my name," my nature. Jesus is teaching us that as we walk in His nature and life, whatever we ask He will do.

God works through His nature in us. It is His holiness, His Word and His righteousness. All we must do to see the power of God is simply surrender to Him.

He is my Fortress, Wonderful, Counselor, Mighty God, Savior, Redeemer, Deliverer, Healer, Prince of Peace, Bread, Meat, Drink, Light of the World, Captain of the Host, the Truth, the Way, the Life, the Alpha and

Omega.

He is "I am," a Shield, a Consuming Fire, Rock of my Salvation, the Most High, Holy One, Lamb of God, Good Shepherd, King of Glory, King of Kings, Diadem of Beauty, Faithful Fountain of Living Waters, Friend, Comforter, the Author and Finisher of Faith.

"He leadeth me in the path of righteousness for His name's sake."

Chapter Seven—
Though I Walk Through The Valley Of The Shadow Of Death, I Will Fear No Evil

David said, "yea though I walk through"… David knew there were trials in life that we must walk through. If we run from adversity, we will never learn spiritual warfare. If we run in fear, we will never develop faith. All things can work together for our good if we trust the Lord with our circumstances.

The attacks of the enemy are not God's perfect will for our lives—that is not His best for us. However, in the attack, if we look to God, He will reveal a means of escape and work all things together for our good.

The test is that we must walk through these tough times. If we are faithful to walk through each situation, we learn about God's way, we hear His wisdom, we witness His power, we allow Him to use us and we grow in faith.

Have you ever tried to tear a wasp's nest apart? The wasp makes the nest strong to protect its young. As the little wasp is growing it is sealed in a compartment of the nest. The nest hangs upside down. As the wasp reaches maturity it begins to tear its way out of the nest. Once the wasp tears out of the nest, it uses its wings to fly. The wasp is able to fly because of the strength it gained working to get free from the nest. To remove the struggle would result in a weak wasp that would fall to the ground and die.

Our faith is strengthened in our struggle—if we allow God to empower us to walk through it—even if it means walking through the valley of the shadow of death.

Death is somewhat scary because we are only familiar with what we experience on this side of death. Death is like a door to a room where we have never entered, so we are left to wonder what we will encounter when we walk through that door.

For many of us, we do not think about death very often—however, when a friend or family member dies many questions usually surface. Why? Why did they have to die? Why do some good people die while evil people get to live? Why did they die so young? Why didn't God save their life?

Just as we question death, we then begin to question our own existence, asking things like, "What is my purpose? Why am I here? How do I find fulfillment?" The purpose of all of these questions is to lead us to "The Answer" who is the Good Shepherd.

James 4:14 states that life is but a vapor; it is like steam hitting the atmosphere—you see it for a moment and then it is gone. We must respect life and always be grateful for the breath we breathe.

Death is merely a doorway into the eternal. We are made in the likeness and the image of God. We are

Spirit and will live eternally either in the presence of God or separated from His glory, which the Bible calls the second death.

Meditation for Today

When I was a little boy playing in my yard, I sometimes saw planes flying in the sky. On some days, when a plane was flying low between my yard and the sun, it cast a large shadow. As I watched the shadow flying toward me I imagined that I could jump on the shadow and it would take me to faraway places. I was never afraid because it was just a shadow. Now, had the plane flown through my yard, I could have been hurt or killed, but I never felt the shadow.

The Shepherd is with us as we walk through the valley of the shadow of death. The reason we fear no evil is because the Shepherd is leading us and He will protect us. He is moving on our behalf even in the things we cannot see. Death is only a shadow we pass through to move into a world that exists in the presence of a God of all glory. A shadow is a barrier to the light. Once we walk through the barrier we will see Him face to face and know Him in all of His fullness and glory.

Chapter Eight— For Thou Art With Me

"For Thou Art With Me." What a comforting thought that no matter what we face in life we can be confident that God will be with us. He has promised never to leave or forsake us (Hebrews 13:5).

David faced many hardships in his lifetime. As a young boy he faced a giant in battle. For him, this was the foreshadowing of living a life of adversity. In Psalm 140 David cried to be delivered from an evil man. In Psalm 59 he prayed to be delivered from violent men. In Psalm 142 he hid from both Saul and his army who were seeking to kill him. In Psalm 109 David dealt with hateful slanderers. In Psalm 61 David was overwhelmed and turned to God once again.

God is always there to hear our cry. The Bible states that He knows our thoughts afar off, which means before we can form our thoughts to speak, God already knows what we need.

God is omnipresent, which means He is at all places at all times. That is why the whole earth is full of His glory. Sometimes we are so overwhelmed with what we are going through we fail to realize that God is present to help.

That is why we must walk by faith and not by sight. Jesus said, "Blessed are the pure in heart for they shall see God" (Matthew 5:8). When our relationship with Him is right and our heart is pure, we can see God in all things.

David was overwhelmed many times but he always reminded himself that he was not alone, for God was with him. At times he was so aware of God's presence that he realized he could never hide from God.

In Psalm 139:7-12, David writes:

"Whither shall I go from thy Spirit? or whither shall I flee from thy presence? If I ascend up into heaven, thou art there: if I make my bed in hell, behold, thou art there. If I take the wings of the morning, and dwell in the uttermost parts of the sea; Even there shall thy hand lead me, and thy right hand shall hold me. If I say, Surely the darkness shall cover me; even the night shall be light about me. Yea, the darkness hideth not from thee; but the night shineth as the day: the darkness and the light are both alike to thee."

He is the God who is there. God was with Joseph in the pit, the prison and in the palace. He was with Ruth in a land of famine. He was with Jacob as he fled for his life. He was with the three Hebrew children in the midst of the fire. He was with David and He continues to be with us.

There are times in our lives that we do not sense or feel God's presence, but that does not mean He left us. When a Good Shepherd watches over His flock there are times He is right in their midst. He speaks to them and calms them. There are even times when He carries them on His shoulder so they can smell His scent and know Him.

There are other times when the Shepherd is watching over the flock from the hillside. He is watching for wild animals seeking to prey on the sheep. He stays attentive from a distance. His love is the same. His care is the same even though the flock cannot smell, hear or see him.

Sometimes our Chief Shepherd is the "Most Nigh God," other times He is the "Most High God"; however, in both circumstances, He is still God.

Meditation for Today

Many people become angry with God and feel that He deserted them when they needed Him most. What they are really saying is God did not rescue them the way they thought He should. In our immaturity we set expectations for God that He never promised to meet.

God has established laws and principles that even He will not violate. Though He is God and can supersede the laws, He also respects the free will of man. Many bad things happen as a consequence of the choices of man.

For example, God has established a law of gravity. What goes up must come down. If a man jumps from the top of a twelve-story building and dies, will we say it is God's fault because God had the power and ability to rescue the man?

God does love us and will never leave us. He is ever present. He is not the policeman of the world determined to make people live right and make right choices. People have a free will and many abuse it. There will be justice one day. For now, know that God will be with you and wants to help you find healing for your hurt....For thou art with me.

Chapter Nine—
Thy Rod And Thy Staff
They Comfort Me

The terms "rod" (or "branch," used at times for beating) and "staff" ("support of every kind") were used interchangeably in the original Hebrew. In this text, it was used by the shepherd for several things: as a weapon to defend the sheep, and also to comfort the sheep. The Bible also records that the shepherd counted the sheep as they passed under the rod.

Probably one of the most famous rods belonged to a shepherd named Moses. There was a day when Moses was on the back side of the desert watching over his father-in-law's flock. It was on this day that Moses had an encounter with God. We must realize that God can reveal Himself in the routine of our day. Such an encounter—in the midst of the ordinary—can become a defining moment that will change our lives forever.

God asked Moses, "What do you have in your hand?" Moses was holding a simple shepherd's staff, a rod. To a shepherd his staff represented his identity and the sheep he owned. Sometimes shepherds would carve their lineage on the staff to represent their tribe, their people and their nation.

Moses' staff represented his strength and his identity; it was what he leaned on when he needed help. God told Moses to throw it down, to give it up. You must understand Moses had given up so much already. He gave up a life in Pharaoh's palace, and he gave up a place among the ruling class to identify with his people. Fleeing for his life he became a shepherd. Now all he had was a staff, and God asked him to give it up.

If we are to be full of God we have to empty our self life. We must die to self, lose our identity and give all to God. Moses had to let go of everything before God could or would use him.

As a young man Moses wanted to deliver his people out of bondage—wanting to shepherd over them. Yet, now he found himself as a shepherd over sheep that he did not own in a desolate, forsaken desert.

When Moses laid down his staff, he was laying down his dream and identity; yet, in doing so, his plan became God's—he threw the staff down as the rod of Moses and picked it up as the rod of God.

The staff used to represent a shepherd and a few sheep; now it represented the authority of the King of Glory and His Kingdom.

The power and authority of God found in the rod was displayed when Moses struck the Nile River with the rod and it turned to blood; when he stretched the rod over the waters and Egypt was plagued with frogs; when he struck the dust and a plague of gnats rose up; when he stretched it toward heaven and fire and hail came down; when he waved it in the air and locusts filled the land and when he stretched the rod out and the Red Sea parted.

Moses moved in authority with demonstration of the power of the universe.

Meditation for Today

The Bible states, "Whoever finds his life will lose it, and whoever loses his life for my sake will find it" (Matthew 10:39; NIV). As we lose our self life, we receive the very life of God. But if we try and live in our self life, we lose the Zoë or the abundant life of God.

What do you need to let go of today? What are you holding on to? If you lay it down God will let you pick it up with power.

Moses fulfilled his life's dream: he became the shepherd of Israel and led them out of bondage to a promised land.

The rod and staff of God protect and comfort us. His rod of authority chastens and corrects us. His discipline fashions us to be all that we can be in Him. His staff pulls us from the snares of life and brings us to a safe place. Thy rod and thy staff they comfort me.

Chapter Ten—
Thou Preparest A Table Before Me In The Presence Of Mine Enemies

The word "preparest" proclaims that God does all the doing and we do all the receiving. That is the type of Covenant that we walk in with God. Man can never become holy or righteous in his own ability. Salvation is not of works lest any man should boast.

When God made covenant with Adam, Adam was merely dust of the earth until God breathed upon him and gave him life. When God made woman, He put Adam to sleep so he could take no credit in her creation. It was God that killed the animal and clothed Adam and Eve after they had sinned.

When God made covenant with Abraham He put Abraham to sleep. We witness this with Moses, Israel, David, and then in the New Testament where Jesus made a new covenant by becoming the Lamb of God, slain for our sins. Again it was God doing everything to make covenant with man. Jesus said "No man can take my life from me, I lay it down and if I lay it down I have power to pick it up again" (John 10:18 Author Paraphrase).

Every good gift comes from above. God says that He will supply all our needs according to His riches in glory through Christ Jesus (Philippians 4:19). Everything that we need is found in Christ. Jesus said, "I am the Bread of Life" (John 6:35), I am meat, and I am living water.

God prepares a table for us to feast. He satisfies our soul.

And notice, God serves us in the presence of our enemies. Remember, "...we do not wrestle against flesh and blood, but against principalities, against powers, against the rulers of the darkness of this age, against spiritual hosts of wickedness in the heavenly places" (Ephesians 6:12-13; NKJV).

"The weapons of our warfare are not carnal but mighty through God to the pulling down of strongholds" (2 Corinthians 10:4). There is a spiritual enemy in a spiritual conflict, which means we must fight in a spiritual realm. Again, God must do all the doing. We only have power because God is All-Powerful.

Exodus 14:14 announces, "The Lord will fight for you and you shall hold your peace" (NKJV).

The people we come in conflict with each day, especially those who attack and try to destroy us, are often energized by a spiritual demonic force. The enemy in the spirit realm energizes and feeds anger and hatred to people living in the earth realm.

The mystery of deception is when a deceived man does not know he is deceived. It takes truth to expose a lie. Truth is light and when the light is turned on in the darkness, men will move to do one of two things: they will either run to the light or they will despise the light and try to turn it off.

The devil attacks us through people because he is trying to turn off the light of Jesus shining through our lives. Satan knows that light in our lives is truth that will set captives free from his bondage.

This is why Jesus commands us to love our enemies, do good to those who hate us, bless those who curse us and pray for those who spitefully use us (Luke 6:27; Author Paraphrase).

The love Jesus uses in this statement is agapé love. This is not a human love; it can only come from God. There will be people who come in and out of our lives that we will not be able to love in our own heart of compassion. God's love has to surpass our feelings, emotions and our logic.

Meditation for Today

Picture yourself as a conduit or water pipe that is connected to the heart of God. The love of God flows to you so He can flow through you.

However, you have the control of the faucet valve. You can choose to turn it on and release the blessing or you can be bitter and unforgiving and withhold the blessing.

If God desires to touch someone by using our lives, who are we to refuse? Once we were enemies of God but someone allowed His love to flow to us and set us free.

Knowing God as the God of battles allows us to be at peace, sit at the table He has prepared for us and feast in the presence of our enemies.

Chapter Eleven—
You Anoint My Head With Oil

David was anointed as King of Israel. The Bible does not state he was made King or he studied to be King, nor was it because he understood Kingdom protocol. The Bible simply states David was anointed to be King.

The sacred anointing of David was a ceremony of dedication. In Old Testament times objects and people were anointed, set apart, separated from the world and separated unto God to do His will.

To reinforce the role of God in Israel's affairs, the Kings of Israel did not wear elaborate crowns like kings among the heathen nations but were instead crowned with an anointing from on high.

I Samuel 16 records the act of Samuel, the Prophet of the Lord, anointing David. All of David's brothers were big men that stood tall, but Samuel walked past those brothers that looked like Saul in outer stature and anointed the least likely one.

Men look on the outward but God looks at the heart (I Samuel 16:7). If you lack integrity, servanthood and other character qualities, you will never be able to stand up under a God-sized blessing.

Samuel took the horn of oil and anointed David in the presence of his brothers. And from that day on the Spirit of the Lord came upon David in power.

Just a few chapters earlier, in I Samuel 10:1, we find Samuel anointing Saul as King. The people cast lots and chose Saul as King. When Samuel anointed him he did not use a horn of oil, he used a vial (a man-made bottle or bowl).

What was the difference? The vial was man-made. A man-made position runs on man-made power. The horn came from a God-made animal. The horn represented maturity, a process of growth and preparation. A God-made position runs on God-given Power.

God empowers us for service. He anoints us before He appoints us.

Noah was anointed to build a boat. Moses was anointed to deliver Israel. David was anointed to be King. Jesus was anointed to be the Christ, the Savior of the World.

The word "Christ" is not the last name of Jesus. "Christ" means "the anointed one and his anointing."

The purpose of the anointing is to provide and equip us to have a quality of life above and beyond the natural man. The anointing mixed with the natural creates something supernatural.

Immaturity is found in believers that look like, talk like and think like a natural man. They need to be disciplined to grow into Christ because the anointing of "Christ in you" will overshadow that which is natural.

Satan does not care if you serve, pray or go to Church. He just does not want you doing anything with the anointing. He knows the anointing breaks the yoke of bondage. Anything we do apart from faith and the anointing is merely religious.

The Bible mentions those that have a form of godliness but no power in their lives. It will not help people if all they see is godly, but powerless, you. But, you change the world when they see "Christ" the Anointed One in you.

Meditation for Today

God does something on the inside before anyone sees Him on the outside.

Jesus was the Christ, the Anointed One, because He was set apart for the mission of saving the world from sin.

God anoints you to do something.

Jesus said: "The Spirit of the Lord is upon me, because he hath anointed me to preach the gospel to the poor; he hath sent me to heal the brokenhearted, to preach deliverance to the captives, and recovering of sight to the blind, to set at liberty them that are bruised, To preach the acceptable year of the Lord." (Luke 4:18-19)

God has anointed us to represent His authority on the earth. To do exploits in His name.

You anointest my head with oil.

Chapter Twelve—
My Cup Runs Over

The cup is a symbol of covenant. Throughout the Old and New Testaments, each time a covenant was made, they would seal the vow with a memorial meal. This is when they would break bread, eat it and drink the wine.

In the Hebrew economy, when a young man and young maiden wanted to marry they would first have to be engaged. It began by the young man first visiting the girl's parents. The man would tell the parents of his intention and then ask their permission and blessing upon the future couple.

Once they agreed, the young man and the girl's father would negotiate a price for the bride. In that day the women worked hard. They would rise early to get wood for the fire. They made meals that sometimes required them to kill, clean and cook before sunrise. They worked in the house and in the fields.

If the parents had all girls and no boys, that meant as the girls got older, married and left home, workers would have to be hired to replace them. So the father would negotiate a price of the worth of his daughter.

Once the price was agreed upon a meal was prepared and celebrated. In that day the engagement was more serious than the marriage ceremony. If a couple broke an engagement it was looked upon as a divorce and disgrace to the families.

After celebrating with the family, the young couple would get alone and have a covenant meal. They broke bread together and each said that the bread was a representation of their life. As they ate together it was symbolic that they were one.

Then they took the cup and said that it represented their life's blood. As they drank together they vowed their love and promised their hearts to each other.

Before a young man could marry he had to prepare a dwelling for himself and his intended bride. As wages were very low, it could take many years to build a house. In many instances, the groom would add a room to his father's house and, when it was complete, he would come for his bride.

As they came to the close of the covenant meal the young man would give the cup to the girl and say, "keep this while I am away preparing a place to lodge. On the days you feel I will not return, take this cup out and remember the vow of promise we have made today." Then she would wait anxiously for his return, not knowing the time or the hour.

What a beautiful picture of Jesus. He came to our house, planet earth, and paid a price for us by giving His Life. He had a covenant meal with His disciples at the Last Supper. Jesus said I will not partake until we have the marriage supper of the Lamb in heaven.

In the Gospel of John, Jesus tells the disciples, "I am going now to the Father's house to prepare a place for you. If I go I will come again and receive you unto myself; that where I am there you may be also" (John

14:2; Author Paraphrase). The Body of Christ awaits her bridegroom. We look with anticipation for His return, not knowing the time or hour.

We honor the Lord's Supper and as often as we partake, we do it in remembrance of Him— remembering what He did by dying on the Cross…what He is doing as we daily walk with Him…that He is coming again and we will dwell with Him forever in a face-to-face relationship.

The covenant cup is a symbol of God's love for all men. It is inclusive of all blessings, all promises, all grace and glory, abundant life here and now and eternal life forever more. It is too much for me to comprehend; it is above all that I can ask or think. Our eyes have not seen, neither have our ears heard nor has it entered into our minds what God has in store for us.

"My cup runneth over."

Chapter Thirteen—
Surely Goodness And Mercy Shall Follow Me

Psalms 33:5 states that, "The earth is full of the goodness of the Lord." The goodness of the Lord is more than an act of compassion. It is more than a gesture of kindness; it is the essence of who He is. In creation, everything that He created was good because it manifested out of His very being. Creation and life came forth as He spoke and that which was invisible in Him, but very real, became visible and very tangible.

The original meaning in our English language for "God" is "Good." When the people called Jesus "Good Teacher," His response was, "…Why do you call me good? No one is good but one, that is, God" (Mark 10:18).

The goodness of God saturates all that He creates and rules over. God created us in a way that we can see with our eyes. God's goodness lets us see color, dimensions, dreams and imagination by faith. Our hearing allows us to enjoy music, sounds of nature and loved ones sharing appreciation.

Though we must eat to survive, God added taste buds that burst with flavor and allow us to enjoy new discoveries of taste. We could live in dark caves but God blesses us with a creation of a beautiful environment of self-sustaining color, sound, smell and textures with each day, beginning with a fresh new sunrise and ending in a majestic sunset of vibrant hues.

Psalms 136:1 says, "O give thanks unto the Lord; for He is good: for His mercy endureth forever." The goodness of God is coupled with His mercy. When God told Moses to hide in the cleft of the rock and He would allow His goodness to pass before Moses (even though no man could see God and live), the mercy of God allowed Moses to experience the goodness of God.

Man was created out of the goodness of God. However, man was given a free will to choose his own way. When man sinned against the holiness of God and was separated from God's goodness, it was God's mercy that redeemed the relationship. If a man chooses to repent, God's mercy makes a way of escape and invites man to enter into the goodness of God.

When Adam sinned against God, he was cast out of Paradise. When God separated himself from Adam, it was the most loving thing God could have done—a sovereign act of His mercy. If Adam would have stayed in the presence of God in his state of sin, mankind would have been annihilated. Ungodliness cannot exist in the presence of holiness, for our God is a consuming fire.

When God came to the mountain to meet with Moses, everything that was not pure was burned by the holiness of His presence. That is why God had Moses put barriers at the base of the mountain that even the unclean animals were forbidden to touch the mountain of God. That is why the angel of the Lord told Moses in the desert to remove his shoes. Moses was standing on holy ground because of the presence of a Holy God.

We could not fully enjoy the goodness of God without His enduring mercy. As believers we are blessed that both will follow us to ensure we drink in all of the life that God pours out.

Meditation for Today

We must never take for granted the goodness of the Lord found in our lives. There are many great memories and experiences in our lives that witness the goodness of God and how He freely gives to all.

"Surely his goodness and mercy shall follow me."

Chapter Fourteen—
All The Days Of My Life

Psalms 90:12: "So teach us to number our days, that we may gain a heart of wisdom" (NKJV).

We must always remember we are in the world but not of the world. God created us with an eternal purpose in mind. We live in this time frame we call life. In the epistle of James, life is referred to as a vapor.

Compared to eternity, this vapor of life is all we know. To some it may end before their childhood years are over, to some they only live to early adulthood. For those that live a full life it will only be an average of eighty to ninety years.

Ninety years compared to a God with no beginning and no end is the vapor of steam James talks about. Life is short and we should daily be aware of each opportunity to create a beautiful memory, tell someone how much we love them and purpose to make another step toward our destiny.

"The steps of a good man are ordered by the Lord" (Psalm 37:23). God has a plan for each life. In His great wisdom He has planned a life for us that will fulfill us and accomplish His will.

He has entrusted to us a thing called time in which we are accountable, for we are stewards over this time.

If we are to make a mark for Christ to impact the next generation we must have purpose in what we do and in how we live.

Many studies have proven that in each person's lifetime they impact the lives of at least ten people around them. Someone near you is being affected by the life you live. It could be a spouse, children, friends or colleagues. God is using you to play a key role of leadership in their lives and in what they will accomplish in this life.

In Psalm 90:12 Moses prays, "So teach us to number our days." It is wise to have perspective for life and to make life count. Time is a valuable part of life. Yet we are guilty of wasting time, losing time and killing time—terms we use for being non-productive.

If we were to look at the average life span of people we find that on an average people live to the age of seventy-five to eighty years of age.

Take that life span and place it in a twenty-four hour period of time. In other words, look at a clock and see it as the time span of a life.

One o'clock a.m. represents birth and twelve o'clock p.m. represents the end of life. Twelve noon would represent forty years of life. If you are in your fifty's you are in the afternoon of your life. If you are in your sixty's to seventy's, you are in the evening of your life.

This perspective brings the Scripture alive where Jesus states, "I must work while it is day for the night is coming where no man can work" (John 9:4; Author Paraphrase).

Jesus was very conscious of His purpose in the earth and His time in which He would accomplish God's Will.

Jesus replied to Mary's directive at the Canaan Wedding, "My hour has not yet come" (John 2:4; NKJV). The Pharisees wanted to stone Jesus but did not because it was not His time. In the garden of Gethsemane Jesus prayed and said, "The hour is come" (Mark 14:41). On the Cross He cried out, "It is finished" (John 19:30).

Meditation for Today

Never allow the distractions of life to dictate what your life should be. Only you can take control of the time span in your life. God has entrusted you with time; take responsibility and be a good steward.

Drink in life and make each moment count for something and God will bless you all the days of your life.

Do you know what time it is?

Chapter Fifteen—
And I Will Dwell In The House
Of The Lord Forever

God has always established a dwelling place for His glory. In the Old Testament, God had Moses and the children of Israel construct a tabernacle for His dwelling place.

Solomon built a temple for God's presence. The temple was extravagant with gold, jewels and ornate craftsmanship. Though the structure was breathtaking, it was only a type and shadow of a greater dwelling place.

As we move from the Old Testament into the New Testament, John 1:12 reveals that Jesus was the Word and the Word was made Flesh and Dwelt (in the Greek dwelt means tabernacled) among us. And we beheld the glory.

Jesus came to earth to live righteously, die for the sins of mankind and resurrect in power. The redeemed of the Lord become the Church or the dwelling place of the living God.

Jesus became the chief cornerstone. Luke 20:17 states that this is the stone the builders rejected. However, God lays a foundation of Apostles, Pastors, Teachers, Prophets, and Evangelists with the chief cornerstone Jesus, then adds the life of each believer which the Bible refers to as lively stones.

We are the temple of the Holy Spirit. We are the house of Prayer. We abide in Christ and His Word abides in us. In Him we live and move and have our being. We dwell in the presence of the Lord because the Lord's presence dwells in us.

David loved to be in the presence of God. As he worshiped with his harp, David sensed the presence of the Lord.

On cold nights, songs of praise were birthed out of his holy encounters. In that place of worship, divine instruction and affirmation surrounded David like a warm blanket.

David knew that in the presence of God he would set up camp as it was his destiny to dwell in the presence of the Lord forever.

Psalm 90:2 says, "before the mountains were brought forth, or even thou hast formed the earth and the world, even from everlasting to everlasting, thou art God." He is a God with no beginning and no end.

In His presence is fullness of joy because He is joy. He is my refuge and place of safety. We are protected by His strength, directed by His wisdom and surrounded by His love.

Thank God that He has called us out of the darkness into His marvelous light to show forth His praise. We were made in His image and after His likeness. He made us to be His dwelling place and though we lost that position by sin, He bought us back with a price, restored us and built us up to be His Holy dwelling place.

We are the house of the Lord, a holy habitation of His praises, a living sanctuary of His love. We are the house of the Lord and He abides within this House of Praise.

We join with David and say, "We shall dwell in the house of the Lord forever!"

Conclusion

In Jeremiah 30:2 the Lord says: "Thus says the Lord God, the God of Israel: Write in a book all the words that I have spoken to you" (RSV).

It has been an honor to share through this book some of the life changing revelations that I have experienced in the presence of God through devotion, prayer and praise.

My prayer is that this book has opened the eyes of your heart to a new understanding of our Lord, the Good Shepherd—and has provoked you to new thoughts, fresh meditation and to a renewed life of holiness.

To Contact the Author

For Comments or testimony on "Meditations of a Shepherd King," or to request Pastor Ronnie Guynes for a speaking engagement, email:
info@pgministriessite.com

783214

Made in the USA